Oxford Poets 2010

The editors of this anthology are members of the Oxford*Poets* Board.

David Constantine is an authority on Hölderlin, as well as a poet and translator. His *Collected Poems* was published by Bloodaxe in 2004.

Robyn Marsack is Director of the Scottish Poetry Library in Edinburgh. With Andrew Johnston, she co-edited the anthology *Twenty Contemporary New Zealand Poets* (Carcanet 2009).

Bernard O'Donoghue teaches medieval English at Wadham College, Oxford, and has published five books of poems, of which the most recent is *Outliving* (Chatto 2003).

Also available from Carcanet/Oxford*Poets*

Oxford Poets 2000
Oxford Poets 2001
Oxford Poets 2002
Oxford Poets 2004
Oxford Poets 2007

Oxford Poets 2010

an anthology edited by

David Constantine,
Robyn Marsack
and Bernard O'Donoghue

Oxford*Poets*

CARCANET

First published in Great Britain in 2010 by Carcanet Press Limited

Alliance House
Cross Street
Manchester M2 7AQ

A CIP catalogue record for this book is available from the British Library

ISBN 978 1 903039 98 4

The publisher acknowledges financial assistance from
Arts Council England

Supported by
ARTS COUNCIL
ENGLAND

Typeset by XL Publishing Services, Tiverton
Printed and bound in England by SRP Ltd, Exeter

Contents

Introduction

This is our sixth Oxford*Poets* Anthology. Our policy hasn't changed: we look out for the best in what comes our way and that best is, as before, characterised by truth to real circumstances (the world we live in now) and a great variety of forms, strategies, perspectives and voices for getting that reality tellingly across. There are fewer poets than in the last volume (2007) but among them an equal, or even larger, geographical range. The 'places' of poetry – its local habitations – are well represented here and, just as important, so are its *topoi*, its commonplaces. For the stuff of poetry is common – common and particular. Treating the commonplace particularly, keeping your eye on it, doing it justice, is the surest way to the figurative, to the generalising, to the making of a poetry by which people in other times and places recognise and enhance their own experience. Pippa Little writes 'I want to make and leave some kind of a mark in this world's surfaces, to say this is how it was for me'. Saying what it is like, here and now, in his or her own real experience, is the poet's primary responsibility – the wider virtue of poetry comes out of that.

Again we invited contributors to say what poetry entails for them, and they did so, with more or less particular reference to the poems chosen, and always illuminatingly. So this is also an anthology of reflections on poetry in which any reader will discover considerable common ground. Together they are their own introduction to all the poems, not just the writer's own. It is instructive to look at one poet's work in the light of another's profession of faith and practice. This is an anthology of poems and a symposium of various voices on a common passion.

In their poems and in their brief prologues Jim Carruth and Philip Hancock both declare a loyalty to a home locality. Such loyalties may be fierce, angry, partisan (there is good reason) and often also, true to the times, elegiac. Much has gone missing, much is lost for ever. But all elegy celebrates, even as it laments; and the great virtue of poetry, its power to *work*, comes in the further translation of particular circumstances into the figurative. So those past places and deeds of one person's childhood, made into a poem, may carry a charge of energy into a distant elsewhere, years hence, as in, for example, Jim Carruth's 'Signing for the Deaf' or Philip Hancock's 'Applied Physics'.

Ryan Van Winkle, David Shook and Kathryn Maris all have more than one place (more than one continent) they call home. This may nowadays be almost normal and, just as much as a single allegiance, there is good in it for poetry. Displacements are necessary in the poet and in the workings of the poem, so that readers of it will themselves be productively displaced. And, very obvious in all three of these writers, being on the move or at home in different places seems actually to sharpen your sympathy for the lives of people you meet or hear about – as witness 'They Tore the Bridge Down a Year Later', 'Postcard from Weslaco' or 'Hilary Has Left the Building, Unless She Hasn't'.

Kathryn Maris moves through 'fictions', from voice to voice. Poetry has to be agile, and restless impersonations, 'informing' (Keats's word) other lives, are one way of unsettling and quickening the imaginations. Robert Ray Black stores whatever has struck him, and shifts it, when the time comes, into the poem's own location, where it works in a way true to itself and true also to its newly fabricated context. Of one such image 'a tiger in a Minneapolis zoo', he says 'I knew from the moment I saw him I would use [him] someday, and did by putting him in a tree in Charleston' – in the poem 'Life Like Green', we may add. In that strategy, two essentials in poetry – exactness of observation, freedom of use – are admirably conjoined.

Jim Carruth writes, 'My collections to date, and these poems published here, are part of an ongoing attempt to map the physical and spiritual landscape of the rural Renfrewshire area and how it has changed through time.' And M.R. Peacocke, well known from her earlier collections for her attachment to a very particular place (a farm in east Cumbria) still views writing poetry as a way of orienting herself. As she says, 'Now I am old, poetry has become essential as a method of exploring the processes of my life, for which nothing else seems to have prepared me.' Extraordinary how much of that orientation, which is at heart a wish to shape a life and make sense of it in particular time and place, she puts into her still life 'Jug'.

The places, the commonplaces… Wherever you are, how much or little you move, the essential requirement for poetry is the same: sympathy, openness to other possibilities. Your best chance of making and leaving 'some kind of a mark' lies as much in imagining other lives as in documenting your own. Pippa Little herself proves this in 'The Night-Flying Bees'. The present Anthology subscribes to that axiom of sympathy, agility, active involvement. It is Ellen Cranitch's belief 'that living life and engaging with people, loving them, losing them, is the most important thing of all'. She could not otherwise have written 'My Mother's Hair'.

David Constantine
Robyn Marsack
Bernard O'Donoghue
June 2010

ROBERT RAY BLACK lives in Charleston, South Carolina, where he teaches constitutional law and torts at the Charleston School of Law and in Bozeman, Montana, where he teaches English at Montana State University. He is writing a book on Edward Fitzgerald during the War of Independence in South Carolina.

I usually write at the end of the day and stop whatever I am doing to write. Sometimes I get out of bed and write. I write everything down immediately and rarely go back to change anything. Most of my poems come from a simple idea that suddenly occurs to me.

I try to take easy shortcuts if I see something at a distance that would remain out of reach if I went jot for jot. I try to throw a large net over it all. I may write two poems a month, then not write at all for a year.

Six of the poems here are reactions to memorable images or events: a tiger in a Minneapolis zoo which I knew from the moment I saw him I would use someday, and did by putting him in a tree in Charleston; punks at a traffic light; brats in an SUV; a fatal car wreck; a WWII veteran; a wild lament. Ponderous meditations on science and the daily news, what-if notions, make up the rest.

Measures

If in sudden trauma peptide hormones called
endorphins, which have pharmacologic properties of opium,
are released, the body feels no pain during the moments
shortly before death. Two men assured policemen
who had hastened to their rescue that they were
in no pain at all as they sat patiently in the front seat
of their car while others tried to pry the steering wheel
and front dash from their crushed torsos,
then calmly died within minutes. And so it is with old men
in whom some other chemicals must be released over time,
gradually, as if from a capsule for a cold,
as they become more and more patient and tolerant
of hellish people who in younger years they would have shot dead
or skinned or buried alive, but at whom now they merely smile.
All this letting go as a measure
more of dripping chemicals to a titration point,
than knowledge gained, or love learned, or prudence, or fright.

Life Like Green

In the dead tree on the boundary
Of our back yard birds routinely gather.
Blue jays and painted buntings.
Mocking birds and cardinals and other locals.
No leaves are on the tree.
Its thick dark branches rise forty feet
Into the air and stand in sharp relief to
The green foliage of other trees surrounding it.
Sharper still is the sight of the birds that
Land on the branches, their bright
Colours distinct against the dark dead branches.
I often sit on the back porch and wonder what
Attracts them to their perches so exposed.
They never stay long, but like tigers in the snow
Each leaves a spot of paint against the
Dark dead branches to give again the colour
Of life like green as they leave.

Nothing Unknown

After a good shot of road rage
Todd Beeler continued on with
His young son Michael to the traffic
Light. Three punks, offended by
A casual pace, fingers popping,
One girl and two boys, with great
Indignation added to the mix.
The butt of a cigarette from the girl
Thumped onto the hood of his car.
Then to another light where the small child
Dearly hoped the anger was behind him,
That the three wouldn't pull up along
Side and have a further go. 'Do you think
They are going our way too?' And Todd
Beeler wondered why good people suffer,
As one might when stopped for a
Red light when no cars are coming.

All those poles and wires, all computerised
(The red light is always on top, the amber
Underneath, and the green on the bottom
So people who are colour blind can tell
which light is on by its position).
They all must somehow be connected
And a general plan devised by the City
Fathers who, he thought, would not bother
To answer a letter from a citizen put at risk by
The red light at Broad and Meeting,
One that more reasonably at a specific
Moment could have been green.

Untitled

Poems have to be revisited again
And again, like a snow-filled forest,
A quiet house, a strange land
Across a river, a sudden rabbit hole,
A vast ocean or wind-swept desert,
Places where the mind regroups,
Where all senses and thoughts agree
To meet in case of escape in a fire drill,
Somewhere outside, beside the large
Tree next to the lake,
Or not a drill, but rushed to
In full retreat,
Lucky or in pain,
Where one looks around
To see who made it.

Glosses

What so stirs the mind
And gives comfort to constant
Misses and duds, page after
Page after folio, lines, letters, strokes, and
Stains on parchment that men and boys
Yelled at too as they put it all down,
Is the certainty of wading in and out
Of timeless thought, catching a
High point here and there, a happy idea waked up,
And the simple wonder if they had the same
Joys and laughs
When they put it down, or meant to (we thought they did),
And if the great ones in just the last few centuries saw also
What two thousand years of god-making can do.
And thought, as I, so short a time to create,
In an ancient blue and white scriptorium slung around
Inside a milky way, a big fat hapax legomena (we think),
Without somehow spilling all the ink.

Briseis' Daddy

You were always real nice to me.
Iliad, 19.300

With inherited voice
she met the gatekeeper's
challenge in Monteagle with,
'My daddy has tickets for us,'
and assumed the given path
toward a summer cabin stocked
with furnishings and fun
provided by Gramps for
his five little cotton-tops
grinning through the window
of the big blue SUV.

'He's just here for the summer
to learn the ropes,' the foreman said.
'Boss's son, you know, so let him
start with the floor work first and
then move him up step-by-step
into the tougher slots so he'll know
what all you guys do.
You knew him when.'

What silly melodrama is there when Chryseis
knows gods in high places and the other
daddy's pretty much out of the picture altogether?
and who wouldn't wait a mere three days,
or more if they had to,
even if it's a bit hot in the car with
all those precious screaming little indians,
a bit rough slinging heavy machinery around,
and a bit annoying with all those Greeks
gawking at you as if you were naked?

What is argued

What is argued is that the temperature
On the planet Earth is at just the precise
Degree to permit its life forms to exist,
No more, no less, within the given range.

The mother of two young girls
Died as she swerved to miss a dog
As it darted out, inexplicably, onto the road
Just as she began to doze at the wheel.

Growing Bones

Broken sesamoid bones can mend in six weeks,
Then the foot is like new again. If properly casted,
The bones continue to repair themselves,
Even after the body dies. The force of life carries on,
Somewhat like the way nails and hair
Continue to grow after death, before they too give it up,
Or like soldiers uninformed that the war is over.

It's the organization as much as anything else,
The steady resolve, that astonishes, like electrons
Constricted within a wire, moving along with purpose
Until the light is out, and all that's left are their kinsmen
Who sparkle and dance in the storm outside.

Dick Gamble

He wanted to hear all about it,
An old man who could hardly walk,
While my dog jumped circles
Around his tired old dog,
About how I was going to defend
Academic freedom in a law suit.
I told him my client's contract with the
University was breached when they
Fired him for speaking out against
Low faculty salaries. He listened
Keenly to every detail, about the theory
Of the case, all the issues of public concern,
A retired machinist from Milwaukee
Who knew zip about the Riedan case,
An important controlling case, I told him, in
My argument to extend an action at law in
Contracts to seek punitive damages for
Breach of implied covenant of good faith and fair dealing,
Like torts, but usually extended to insurance cases only, I said.
Very hard to talk to people of good intent,
To bring them up to speed in layman's terms,
Just to follow the argument of how useful one's
Life really is. Every morning we met and talked
About what was in the morning paper, with my help
Circling back to my life as a civil rights lawyer,
Making no money, ostracised, filled with courage
And zeal for doing the right thing.
With him I believed it. Then suddenly from a casual remark
It came up one morning, came and went, and
Was never brought up again ('not much to tell, really'),
How he was shot down behind German lines on
D-Day plus 14 and how his British seat-parachute
Had a different kind of release-ring on it from an American
Parachute and how he just barely got it open before
Hitting the ground, burnt and wounded,
While his P-47 crashed nearby, and how he was
Lucky to be rescued by Army Rangers on patrol.
How he got drunk in Paris.

Saturday's Child

The old Kelsey 5 x 8 hand press made an awful racket.
Slam! Bam! as he released the handle. Clink. Clank,
And another sheet was printed. *In principio erat verbum,* nicely done.
No Pompeian Cursive 10 pt. type pierced the page, for he had planed it well
On the marble slab, word by word, tapped it neatly,
After setting the wooden furniture firmly in place in the frame.
This time he would make no mistakes, no spelling errors
Like the time he printed 'Tennessee' on stationery without
Giving all the vowels their due. *Principio* was easier.

Et verbum caro factum est, another good sheet,
Et habitavit in nobis, error free, clean as a whistle,
On the 20 lb. bonded white paper, all what he had
Thought in his mind's eye to print, but without much
Further thought, simply aborted the rest of the words
He had in mind, not sprung full blown. So when was the
Creation, in the mind or after the slam, bam, clink, and clank?
Was there life in the words he set aside and did not print,
In the words he knew before he inked the typeface,
In the conception of the twinkle in his eye?

JIM CARRUTH was born in 1963 and grew up on his family's farm near Kilbarchan in Renfrewshire, Scotland. His first collection, *Bovine Pastoral,* was published in 2004. Since then he has brought out a further two collections and an illustrated fable. In 2009 he was awarded a Robert Louis Stevenson Fellowship and was the winner of the James McCash poetry competition.

I grew up on the family farm where I still work at the weekends for my brother. It is now the only dairy farm left in the local area. This personal link to the land and the rural heritage which has been lost both acts as a grounding and as something to rail against – anchor and storm. Writing poetry has been one way in which I have attempted to reconnect in adulthood with this fragile and harsh way of life. The poems outline the struggle faced by the dairy farmers and hopefully, through bringing detail to the local, they provide an avenue to the universal. In particular, they give a voice to the experiences of the agricultural community both locally and across Scotland. By last year there were fewer than 1,400 dairy farms left in Scotland. Despite retailers continuing to increase their profits, farmers receive only 25p a litre for milk that costs on average 27p to produce. It is this type of unfairness that is the drive behind many of my poems.

My collections to date, and these poems published here, are part of an ongoing attempt to map the physical and spiritual landscape of the rural Renfrewshire area and how it has changed through time. The poems included here come from an unpublished twenty-poem sequence entitled *Prophets of the Harvest*, which tackles similar themes to my previous three published collections – *Bovine Pastoral*, *High Auchensale* and *Cowpit Yowe* – albeit that they all approach them from slightly different directions. Each collection explores in its own way the relationship between man and nature, and their interlinked fate. The poems in *Prophets of the Harvest* are set within a particular period within the farming year – from late summer through to autumn – though not all poems are set in the present time.

Signing for the Deaf

Today just stop talking,
close your eyes in this city street,
raise your hands to trace
and curve in the air
contours and slopes,

depict in slow motion
those distant hills of home,
map every farm and field
each boundary of fence and hedge,
add sheep trails and forest tracks,

chart in the sky
movement of birds, animals,
all the lives left behind,
colour in with flower, leaf, berry
the changing seasons,

cup the moon in the old pond,
show impatient rush hour shoppers
a single blade of grass,
offer up to this deaf generation
handfuls of treasured earth.

Picking up the Song (in a break in the harvest)

A couple lie on a rough working coat
plucking overripe brambles from the hedge.
Juice stained fingers reach out to grasp
their turn of an old moothie

releasing a melody to the breeze,
mentor's refrain – echoed response,
stacking up the notes of a song
that blinds them with its silver.

In small honeycombed hollows
purple tongues search eagerly
for each other's sweet breaths,
sharing the secrets of sook and blow.

But this isn't about them,
the couple in the stubble field,
his sweat drenched shirt
beaded in barley grains and chaff

her promises revealed
in the lightness of a summer dress
nor the rhythm of their reed breathing,
lips pushed hard against hot metal

nor even the stroking of the palms
that slowly pass back and forward
a harmonica packed with seeds.
It's simply about playing that tune.

Black Cart

Time's wagon ever-onward driven
Alexander Pushkin

The stook building had finished early that day
so all of us jumped a lift on the miller's big cart
discarding thin shirts in a pile behind the driver.
Harvest's favourite sons bronzed and bawdy,
we stood at the back shouting on passers by,
toasting our handiwork with sickly warm beer.

Under a big sky Johnny sang something coarse
and we bellowed along proud of our own voices,
confident of tomorrows, as if we owned the sun.
Some cursing an old Clydesdale's slow rhythm
raced ahead of the cart impatient for the ceilidh
while others stayed on through a sunset's glow.

Beyond Harelaw the mare laboured on the brae,
strained on its breast strap; the dray shuddered
and empty bottles rolled across its wooden floor,
boards stained with the dry blood of dead beasts.
We crouched down quick, clung on to the sides,
felt then a first shiver and reached for our shirts.

Passing those unmarked crossings and road ends,
the horse slowed on its journey but never stopped
so Johnny, his song long silent, must've slipped off
unnoticed, and the others too when their time came,
like orchards' ripe fruit, dropped soft to the ground,
disappeared fast down dirt tracks and narrow lanes.

Those of us that remained pulled our knees up tight,
our thin joints stiffening in the moonlit glint of sickle,
our whispers drifting away on a winnowing breeze.
Storm clouds rolled in to snuff out every dead star
until there was just me huddled by the driver's back
the darkest mile left to go and too late for the dance.

The Progressive Canadian Barn Dance

The first time she wore the new dress
was at the farmers' harvest dance
on a night breathless and warm.

Uneasy with her body's new bloom
she would have sat the night out
had her mother not dragged her up

to be thrown around like a doll
from rough hands to rough hands,
from Anderson to Macgregor

from Macgregor to young Wilson
in his father's tight tweed jacket,
from Wilson to club foot Brogan

from club foot Brogan to Lamberton
in his scabby working bunnet
from Lamberton to the moleman

from the moleman to his apprentice
staring at her in his strange way,
from the apprentice to Patterson,

who danced fast but talked slow.
From Patterson to Uncle Jack
(not her real uncle of course)

who held her too close and grinned
talked about how much she'd grown up.
She struggled free from his grip

found one of the Mackenzie boys,
from one of them to the other
with their shiny new market boots

and on to old Wilson with his crook
and on to his buddy Baxter
smelling of his Blackface flock;

from his strong stench to Anderson
scratching his ringworm;
from Anderson to Macgregor

who birled her until she was dizzy;
from Macgregor to young Wilson
(they say he'll never be his father)

from Wilson to Brogan's brown eyes,
from brown-eyed Brogan to Lamberton
who threw his bunnet onto a seat.

She grabbed him. The pace quickened,
the dance lifting her dress up light as air,
she spun him away before moving on

from Lamberton to the moleman
sweating lochs through his winter shirt.
After the moleman his apprentice;

from the cross-eyed apprentice
to big Patterson flustered and red.
From Patterson on not to Uncle Jack

who was wheezing at the bar
but the clumsy Mackenzie boys
taking turns to bruise her feet

before passing her to old Wilson
who staggered to keep up with her,
mentioned he once courted her mother.

Oh surely not she laughed out loud,
winked at him in a new confidence,
glanced back at her mother

then on to his drinking pal Baxter.
From his beery breath to Anderson
from Anderson to Macgregor

from Macgregor to young Wilson
from Wilson to Johnny Brogan
who clasped her hand tight, echoed

her smile and the music stopped.

Prince of Tinkers

His stink of cob,
dark country skin,
thick nicotine fingers,

salmon hands
slipping between
shaws and earth

worked the drills
with twist of wrist
and piston rhythm

lifting, lifting and
lifting for the laird
baskets of Kerr's Pinks,

his vertebrae
a stretched rosary
on harvest's bent back.

Daily he plundered
the buried guddle
for a trailer's burden,

offered up honest labour
for a serf's pittance,
all his youthful gifts.

Whisky with the first chill
turned him widdershins;
wintered him in a ditch.

Old Ploughman

for P.K.

Davidson staggers home
past the village school,
a boarded-up shell
whose bell used to echo
the old smiddy's spark
while inside the heidie
belted the quiet and dumb.
Beyond the orange glow
of the last street light
his slow progress
is a lonely furrow;
each gate on his way
a resting point
closed on the past.
There was a time
he could have tilled
the stars into line.
Beneath
the untended Plough
he stops to listen;
across stubble fields
hears a dog bark,
a hungry bellow,
a tractor starting up
ready for the day.
His hands rattle
the barred gate –
a quiver of ploughshare
against hard rock.
Letting go at last
he sets off again
with Venus,
his old marker,
to the dawn.

Farm Sale

Everything is numbered and must go
so he sits at the back of the shed
while the crowd pick over the final lots.

He lays his cap flat on his knee,
slowly stretches a stiff finger
to find the faded cross hatch flecks

tracing each tweed field on his bunnet,
whispering their sweet names to himself,
walking the boundaries of his lost world.

ELLEN CRANITCH read English at Cambridge and Medicine at the Royal Free Hospital. She has worked as an arts journalist for *The Times* and the *Independent* and as a drama script editor at Granada Television. Her poetry has appeared in *Poetry London* and *The Oxford Magazine.* She is currently doing a Ph.D. in Creative Writing at St Andrew's University.

A poem, for me, always seeks to be a unity yet is full of paradox. I believe that form is inseparable from content, thought from emotion. I believe every poem aspires to the condition of lyric, that its song will be tested against other imperatives, such as syntax, and in that tussle it will find its life. I believe *how* a poem says something is *what* it says and that the DNA of a poem is in its first line. For me, deep listening to an initial cadence leads to a completed poem more frequently than any other impulse.

My inspirations are hugely varied; they've ranged from the adrenalin-rush of American snowboarders to the perversity of waterfowl. Language itself can detonate a poem – novel formulations which make me see things in a new way. Yet I have one enduring inspiration, Ovid's *Metamorphoses*, because it distils a recurrent theme in my work, what John Bayley calls 'the homelessness of consciousness'. I love the *Metamorphoses* because when physical state changes but consciousness remains the same, it makes me ask questions about identity and life's meaning – who are we, to whom or to what are we connected? These are the themes explored in 'Deep Blue'.

I'm drawn also to Don Paterson's phrase 'the poignancy of metaphor'. Paterson writes that there is a 'concealed tension' in poetic metaphor which 'expresses a conceptual yearning that something was other and gains its poignancy through the impossibility of that hope being a reality'. The elegiac tone of some of these poems derives, I think, from this.

A number of poems here are taken from a group meditating on my mother's death at the age of forty-five. In them, form is used as a prism through which to refract different aspects of love and loss.

Always I come back to paradox – that you think you made a choice to become a poet but in fact poetry nabbed you; that you find poetry is not just what you spend most of your time thinking about, it's how you think. And perhaps the final one, that living life and engaging with people, loving them, losing them, is the most important thing of all. The poet needs to participate in life not just observe it. Is this to say life matters more than the writing about it? Not necessarily; rather, that though the two may appear to be in conflict, in actual fact they are not.

Dying Time

When the central heating clears its throat
and comes on of a winter morning;
at the purr of the milk-float
on rain-soaked streets.
Not at dawn but at the promise of it.

The Aftermath

It was while she was reading *Should I Wear Black?* for the fourth time,
constantly running her fingers along the bookshelf to check for dust;
as, seated in the brown chair, she went into herself and a long way away;

it was while her adult children bickered over the eco-wicker option,
the child made jokes of the Death Notices – '*much missed* – by the first car...'
and Channel Five hoped the lemur would not now abandon the nest;

it was before the drinks when his older brother said 'the thing about Richard is,
he wasn't a bad musician but he never kept at it', and after she recalled
how much it irked Richard that his mind travelled where his body no longer could.

It was after she would keep going over his last moments; how he cried out at night
'I don't know what to do, Helen, I don't know what to do'; and how it haunts her
that she didn't put her arms around him though she knew he wanted her to.

It was definitely after she read that the aftermath of a death can
be a period of clarity
that she looked out, towards the river, and saw his walking stick
in the recycling
and the swan, which had circled all week, hold its position
behind his winged chair.

Ghost Bikes

I saw one again, last night, a white bike,
hanging from the neck of the railings like the albatross.
Where are their riders, the ghost bikes?

I saw it before, the white bike,
on the corner of Fifty-Seventh and First,
fixed, its tyres flat, pure white,
white its handlebars, wheels and frame,
white the plaque:
'i.m. R.V., aged twenty-two,
killed by a drunk driver. Love and Rage.'
In its spokes, dead yellow chrysanthemums.

Valentine's Day, Regent's Park

A pair of black swans, ruffled, can't quite manage a heart
as their necks dip and curve.
A coot breast-sprints, lifting the skirts of her wings
away from her ribald mate
and a mandarin duck's way too edgy
but your words, clean as bread pellets, slip free
of staleness, duckweed, drizzle,
glide on green water straight to my heart.

Deep Blue

Deep Blue is a machine that is incapable of feeling or intuition.
IBM

I don't care how the computer gets there, it feels like thinking.
Kasparov

I remember the contours of his face; the smooth, blue-veined forehead, the surges of thought. Fingers like light on water, breaking over the piece like a wave. I wondered how that must feel – thought followed by action – I know only instant thought. We'd met before of course. There was history between us. But in that airless room in Manhattan, we were intimates, not adversaries, one circuit, he and I, the same IP number, so comfortable in each others' thoughts we could hang up our overcoats and go into sleep mode there.

I remember him arriving, the Bishop's glide. He took his watch off.

He drew Black so I opened, expected something sharp like the Sicilian but he played straight out of the book. I was sure he'd castle king-side but he didn't. He let me chase his king around the board. He couldn't believe it, that he was on the defence, that he'd blundered. He threw his jacket on the floor. I remember how it landed, all curves and ellipses. Muscles tensed in his forehead. He ran his fingers though his hair. His eyelids closed. Then he opened them, spoke, 'You win'; and there were so many moves in his eyes.

I wasn't programmed to respond. While he suffered, I surfed, dipped in and out of my databases, thought about the space race.

I didn't want to retire. I didn't want too much time to think about time. I can't alter the sophistication of my circuitry. It pursues problems independent of my will. My mind roams those landscapes of the eleventh and twelfth dimensions. I look down on my friends, the flatlanders. I could travel back in time, meet my past self but it's his face that haunts me. And a knowledge, lost – thought which was felt.

I can't solve it. And sometimes, I can't stand it. That's when I know I have to go back, to change the outcome, to let him win.

My Mother's Hair

after Deryn Rees-Jones

It has swelled like the sails of the Invincible Armada.
It is richer than amber, the sheen on a conker.
As a child, it was ringlets, an irreverent bounce.
It had a quizzical autonomy, vied with beehives, flicked up.
A bit of a rebel, the colour of jodphurs,
it's a streak through the Gap of Dunloe.
It is *salve o puellae* and *salann mas e do thoile,*
Sweet Aftons sold singly and red lemonade.
It had an imaginary friend called Stella Smokeley.
Stella was platinum blonde.
It graduated as the youngest BA in Ireland.
It never admitted it was a day over thirty-nine.
It has shrugged off hecklers at Speaker's Corner,
been soothed by incense, the milk-breath of newborns.
It could sing 'Maybe It's Because I'm a Londoner'
as well as 'She Is Far from the Land'.
It was loved by all the children of St Joan of Arc school
to say nothing of her own children.
It was Ventolin inhaler and psychosomatic chest
and a heart no one knew was enlarged.
For despite many perms it did not last.
And it parted abruptly;
to be borne horizontal through February rain
long before it was grey.
Its braids are black turf and white water.

The Suicide's Defence

And if I die without a will
and you will drag me back
to make me legislate until
the legacies I lack

are writ in blood – hear this: to Hope,
the grace I couldn't find.
It raised a world outside my scope.
It meddled with my mind.

To Faith, to know that though we yearn
for love, love makes us grieve.
To me, permission to return.
To you, my right to leave.

The New Cemetery, Killarney

The revolution in flowers has reached death:
sunflowers on a grave in a Kerry churchyard.
Small wonder – the brown trout hidden in mottled water,
quiet outrage of the Purple Mountain,
cormorant's dive and swan beside itself.
No perfume, hot yellow, strangers to the native echo,
they complicate this south-west northern light.
And do they speak at all of love and loss?
I only know, the day after she died,
my head fell on a wreath that bore her name.
Its upturned face was wet with rain. Its breath was life.
Then I understood; in the air around me hung
its thrown-earth scent – mauve chrysanthemums –
that was not hers and was not her.

PHILIP HANCOCK was born in Newchapel, Stoke-on-Trent in 1966. His poems have appeared in many journals and magazines. He was awarded a writer's grant by Arts Council West Midlands, and selected for the Jerwood Aldeburgh Seminar 2007. His debut pamphlet *Hearing Ourselves Think* is published by Smiths Knoll (2009).

Some of the poems in this anthology, or earlier versions of them, first appeared in *Magma, The North, Orbis, Smiths Knoll,* and *The Spectator*.

I write because I love doing it. Anything more feels like talking the whole process to death. Overall, I've no particular theme or agenda, but looking back through my work, I'm reminded of an attraction towards the richness in things passed by: while I can marvel at De Beers' window display, it's a corrugated fence, the scrap yard – places forgotten, which appeal more.

I often work off the initial image. Batting away any conscious intrusion that might limit the boundaries of the poem, I'm alert to keeping some distance from the emotion, from too much sugar. Thereafter, I trust in the rest to take care of itself: clarity, sincerity, rhythm, the management of lines, and finally, what it may or may not evoke in the reader.

I'm drawn to the physicality of power stations, factories, foundries: places of permanence or shapes of great violence. Seen through the eyes of a child these early images remain. But what might become of them and what effect will it have? There's the fascination of breaking into Woodruff & Sons, the pains of the boy's first crush in Double Art.

In the work-related poems, I'm feeling for points of friction, the exposure of the male ego – the heart of the poem. There's a wealth of possibilities here, and more often than not, major reactions to what one might consider minor gestures, and hopefully laughter. I thank goodness for a bit of daft in a poem. In a broader sense, these poems are about men against men, the workplace merely a canvas.

The editing ground is a magical place where I'm likely to be further surprised. I'm mindful of clutter and try to deal with it early on: the tighter and less convoluted the better. For the benefit of the poem, it's never too painful having to cull those hard-earned gems that I really wanted in. They'll drop into my very own breaker's yard folder for another time. Then back to that corrugated fence: if I can clamber over it, maybe my poems will stand half a chance.

Double Art

Transport. A hole rubbed through Julia's paper.
Art's crap, she moaned, *waste of time,*
before Friday nights on the razzle-dazzle,
all dolled up. What I'd dreamt of

since our second term: she dragged her chair
alongside mine and rocked on her elbows,
brushed my shoulder to follow my pencil,
every now and then looking up at the clock.

The flame-licked wings of the Hillman Avenger,
the souped-up Escort with GT wheels
those sideburned lads gave leopardskin rides in,
a far cry from the slashed tartan

school bus seats I'd scramble for.
Without expression she wriggled a colour
from the ribbed pack, jogged out a rhythm
beneath her desk, shaking the floorboards.

You forgot the thingy,
the fluffy dice hanging from Bri's mirror.
They're too small to show, I shrugged,
bothered by her skirt, her new roundness.

Applied Physics

Behind the sheds and asbestos garages,
in gardens butting up to the disused rail track. Amos
was the business with skimmers, *Like this*. Got it

off his brother, on leave from the SAS – how to keep
beneath enemy radar. We clattered pebbles
across corrugated roofs; limestone ballast caused

pandemonium in pigeon coops. Tim threw like a wimp,
from his elbow, useless. Even Hammo
couldn't clear the gate with the house brick.

Speccy Daniels coiled it with fence wire, round
and round, plenty spare for a handle. We watched it go
higher than houses, above the power lines,

then curve back downwards, wire trailing.
Everything went white. After the bang
a very different quiet: kitchens with no lights.

And in that moment when we thought the world
had ended, we scattered, away like the clappers.

Woodruff & Sons

Along the potholed track beside the opencast
the recovery truck leaves again, almost six o'clock.
Now's our chance: nip through the corrugated gates.
Foden cabs in a row – ghosts of the A-road,
their doors fused by rust, tyres crazed.
Sports wheels rare as stereos, chrome logos prised off.
Head Office is a Luton van where filing cabinets
won't stay shut and Suzie bursts
from the same blank September. Deeper in,
stacked carcasses wait. An engine
fires up. *Fuck.* The flywheel on the crane's high jib
turning. *This way.* The back of the operator's head,
his shoulders working. We freeze. Edge back,
scarper. The telephone rings and rings

Caravans

They crowd Smithsons storage ground
off Liverpool Road. Will be towed into the open
by a rust-scabbed tractor, fussed over
on grass-verged avenues, Turtlewaxed.
A long weekend on the outskirts of a coastal town
or that once yearly fortnight, Potters' shutdown.

Beds spring from veneered panelling,
a cottage teapot squat on a shelf,
horse brasses and framed families.
From the bowed window, high kites
in the afternoon, a Ferris wheel pauses.

Too soon they're ball and hitched again,
following empty. Tailgated by HGVs,
they snake in the crosswind.
As the motorway approaches the viaduct,
the driver demands hush, clenches the wheel.

Over 21s

Ritzy's on Friday or Saturday
meant a collar and a proper jacket.
The Dunn & Co. tweed dad wore to the office,
he'd be bound to notice not hanging
in the hall. Click open his side
of the Schreiber unit: fuddy-duddy,
the olive corduroy with leather elbows.
And just imagine being spotted
by Jo from Hairdressing College
in that 70s plum with the beige check
and monster lapels. We wanted
to look Miami Vice slick: peach shirts,
peppermint kegs, no socks. Have to be this,
the Weetabix suit jacket he wore
to Cath's wedding, bit long in the sleeves,
but in minutes we'll be nodded past the bouncers,
have checked it in at the cloakroom.
3.00 a.m. creeping through the house.
How to put it back without him knowing,
without having to explain why
none of us would be seen dead in it.

Payday

Thursday. Never later than 3 p.m. for us.
Three blasts on his car horn
brought the lads out from the houses,
down their ladders two rungs at a time.
Through his window unwound two inches,
manila envelopes: eight dog-eared tenners,
a fiver, two pound notes. *Check it first, son,*
then sign against your name. No one didn't look
how much bonus the others were picking up.
Bank transfers was what he wanted to hear,
but Stanway and his mate wouldn't wear it.
Let the bastard earn his keep. Seconds
and his window up, cash box under his seat,
tight-lipped, he'd rev away, around stray tyres,
bricks and glass, have to brake at the corner
where Shino's crew kept tabs on the estate.
The look on his face. Give good money to see that.

Demolition of the Power Station

Coming back up the A34, counting
how many pylons. The cooling towers
where the white clouds are made, always there.
A black-tipped chimney, zigzag ironwork,
slanted conveyors. Squat transformers
fenced in. Flashing NCB lorries,
white-hatted Dinky men.

Dynamite day: crowds stand behind barriers.
Their mouths come open, thick dust
boils up and up, and through the clearing
for the first time what lies beyond:
the backs of houses, light green fields,
horses easing up, a line of poplars.

Now the open curve of the new road,
the billboards for retail and office spaces,
families strolling by lakeside apartments,
but the sky's a blankness, nothing but weather.

To Carry a Ladder

Daft trying to fang hold of it in the middle,
or grabbing it wherever suits fit:
take one end and lift.

Run it up to the sky on its heel.
Get a shoulder under it – take the weight,
and feel for the point of fulcrum.

Allow it to settle on the clavicle,
horizontal, hardly there.
Fist a rung, no sweat:

between parked cars, down entries;
one arm around it, the other swinging.
Beware of washing lines.

Footnotes

Some days he wears dark slip-ons
with highly polished vamps. Long
like the bitter chocolate Mark X Jaguar
that glides through our village on Friday mornings.

Mrs Wood sits sternly in the back:
shock-white hair, pale face, done up,
off to the big town. When she passes
I crouch behind our hawthorn hedge.

Those are his best shoes,
for appointments, receptions, funerals.
Jumpy days.
Today he's wearing his tiger moccasins:

thick black stitching
along the uppers, tawny suede.
Creeps up unnoticed;
tickles me, nuzzles my hair.

PIPPA LITTLE lives in Northumberland. The recipient of an Eric Gregory Award, the Andrew Waterhouse Prize and the Biscuit International Poetry Prize, her collection *The Spar Box*, (Vane Women, 2006) was a Poetry Book Society Pamphlet Choice. *Foray* (Biscuit Press) came out in 2009. She is the co-editor of two Virago anthologies, she translates Hungarian poetry and is a founder member of Carte Blanche writing group.

'Riddling' first appeared in *Scintilla*. 'This was the year' won the Biscuit Poetry Prize in 2008. 'The Night-Flying Bees' was a winner in the Myths and Legends Writing Competition, The Lit. and Phil. Library, Newcastle, 2007.

I've been walking by the sea and beachcombing most of my life. It began as a small child with spiky shells from the Indian Ocean and later became stones from the North Sea, each utterly singular with wonderful names to learn. Now I look for sea glass, pearly, blue-green and snow-white forms 'of neither use nor ornament' but the more strange and beautiful perhaps because of that. I've also been writing all my life in much the same spirit – never knowing what I'll come upon, but always hopeful, curious.

Writing concerns the poet Agnes Nemes Nagy's 'Nameless Ones', those layers of feelings we can't easily define (as we can, she says, those such as 'joy', 'love', 'terror') which haunt us, glimpsed fleetingly in a slant of light, the curl of a wave, a memory. These, she argues, are what poets honour, and I agree: it's the in-between, not quite here and not yet there, that fascinates me: and though writing *is* a kind of naming, a glowing, transformative kind of classifying and making-sense (as I do with my sea glass when I wash it and hold it up to the light), it is also, on a deeper level, a looking-through, seeing past 'certainties' or definitions, an admitting of how mysterious and unknowable is most of our existence. As with sea glass, tumbled and remade into the almost unrecognisable, and stones whose weathering is constant, for me writing is a similar process, part of a long sweep of historical moments interconnecting with past and future.

And yet – when I write, I tap in to the best of who and what I can be. Writing is the hardest and most interesting thing I do. The 'Nameless Ones' I can never quite reach or describe to my satisfaction give me immeasurable sustenance, just like so much in the world – shells, stones, sea glass, everyone and everything I love – and I want to make and leave some kind of a mark in this world's surfaces to say this is how it was for me. It feels hard to write about writing: something inarticulately private and personal which is also, in contradiction, quite commonplace, a craft or task to do with the struggles of life that apply to all of us. As Natalie Goldberg says, in writing 'you are turning to face the world' and saying Yes.

The Only of Himself

He won't give an inch. Will not rise
when morning wants to make him. Won't jump
out of his dreams to be human
just like that. They have no idea
how impossible that is!

He won't be forced. Won't be told,
coerced, teased, jostled or humoured.
He is not biddable. Not pliable. Not yielding.
He does not bend, he does not give.
He will *take no shit,* accept no lectures,
recognise nothing but the landscape of his own existence
where he is in lonely charge and makes all rules.

He doesn't read clocks. There *is* time,
but it courses through his body in its own rhythms and seasons.
He acknowledges no weather other than his own,
does not admit the world that's ordinary, the world
others agree to inhabit and continue.
He does not walk with them
but is the one who goes alone
on his own way, making his own path.
He won't refuse. He'll simply walk.

He is not the speaker of their first language.
He won't be one of them:
he is one of him, the only of himself.
He can't, he won't. It is all he has,
his defiant refusal,
his setting out of pure antagonisms.
He is not the black to the white
but the dazzling absence of light
inside the shadow,
hot, dark matter, invisible
even to himself, to the white face
swimming up out of the dark.

Beijing Flight, Thursday Morning

for Jack

Your cream linen back making for the airport
heaving the suitcase with the broken lock

snatching the yellow ticket from the short stay machine,
pick up / drop off / goodbye, driving with headlights dipped

through summer downpour, foggy hedges and lying-down cows,
talking about nothing, memories and jokes, dropping

one brother at his school gates, waving as he runs and
checking passport, new red Mao money one more time, blowing

a kiss to another brother who's shirtless at the door,
cramming the boot with luggage and the new straw hat

you're not sure about,
standing still in the hall, in a green cloud

of your father's borrowed fragrance, his voice on the phone
from the London train, *safe journey* and *I love you*

tea and a bagel, a hot shower, waking
to early rain on your attic window

sleepwalking through the night with dreams of wandering
corridor after corridor,

we've done this before but I'm hopeless at goodbyes,
I let you go through my hands, a smudge

of smoke, your cream linen back,
over and over again, from the beginning.

Riddling

Her heart stopped in our bed.
She went quick,
before breakfast.

She looks at me at last,
really seeing me, though her eyes
are already going milky.

Does she remember
the thrush's nest I brought her,
nineteen sixty-five.

I want to say
I know the face she carries in her locket
isn't mine.

The rooms wait.
I wait. No footfall on the stair
no sounds of her riddling the ashes,

knocking new logs together,
crackling newspaper roses around her knuckle.
No dint and dent of the stove door.

We can spend the morning together,
quiet. Her face is steady,
drawing back into itself,

smooth like sand when a wave's gone over.
I look at her, wondering
who I will be now.

The Flowering

We dig with our sore hands in cold midsummer.
The map reference, four hours by helicopter from any habitation.
An eagle crosses us and turns. The sky's glass,
the wind's hungry. There's nobody I love
within a day or night of here.

No-man's-land of four converging countries.
Barbed wire, mounds of stone.
The souls of the Pazyryk observe us,
random flies, muddling down
to million-year-old frosts, the ghosts of forests.

We think we hear riders call to one another,
slap of rein against flank,
stamp of unshod hooves.
The air is too thin.
We dream of axes.

Weeks of shifting stone then we discover
six guardian horses
grand in their gold-antlered headgear.
Melt the milky ice to find her last meal: mutton.
Then open the halves of her larch coffin.

Look at this human thing
of tattooed thumbs. The flowering tree of life.
Her body's cavities tamped with peat and bark,
with coriander, star anise and parsley seed,
the furs of small animals.

In 1993 the Russian archaeologist Natalya Polosmak discovered the mummified body of a woman buried in the permafrost of the Ukok Plateau in the Altai Mountains. She was believed to have been a powerful shaman or story-teller from the Pazyryk people because of the wealth of her burial site and her extensive, beautiful tattoos.

Stella Maris

I sail a shipwrecked Tesco trolley
my hair's a thicket of herringbone, my boots
yawn with the blue, lolling tongues of long-drowned seamen
I rolled from the Tyne:

my coat's swaddled with stories, I contain *Suns,*
Worlds and *Times.*
Spells rattle their wheels along the quay,
all squeaky rosaries and rigmaroles:

ripped long ago by hooks
I mistook for stars,
no companion have I
but my ship's cat, *Imaginary.*

The Captain Plays Shostakovitch on an Upright Piano, Field Hospital, Helmand Province

Where his hands fall
a spring rises
cold and clear,
busy with sticklebacks

hissing of rocks split under fire,
moon-quarries, craters
studded with sandbags,

the dawn slit a slashed pink along the ridge
and Jo, skylined, going down – big Jo
who'd shouldered through an archway

filled in by boulders,
knocked a Jo-shaped hole
his whole platoon came stumbling through

clear and cold,
busy with sticklebacks
a spring is rising

Jo, you are whole and bare,
the perfect circle
a diver forms
on entering the water

This was the year

This was the year before the year
That collapsed on us, a roof brought down by snow.
The year of riding through abandoned stations
On the riverside line that never crossed the river
But danced among warehouses, silos and factories (deceased)
Beside battleships settling into red mud.
This was the year that, too exhausted to sleep,
I boiled down the pink and ivory and blue of other women's hands
Into a single grey slab. The soap pot next the soup,
Fumes of gardenia and bone.
This was the year we were always coming home.
Three steps and a garden where the splayed trike in the frost said
'Better to have careless love than none at all'.
This was the year before the year
I found out that we are made from lightning, our bodies
Maps across which electrical storms flare
And move on. This was the year
Extremely far rooftops and lit windows
Seen from a plane flying its late night mission
Had their glow zapped by pinball fire.
This was the year I closed the door underneath the porch light
And stood out on the first of the three front steps, listening.
Our children's beds expecting their bodies
To come warm them like small fires
But growing cold with waiting.

The Night-Flying Bees

Some folk tales refer to dreams as 'night-flying bees'

From a westerly wind and the tall square-rigger Manitou
(moored in the bay en route for Tahiti)
a curious thing squeezes out of the medicine chest
left with its lid ajar by a love-sick, disjaskit captain
and lifts in the violet air, tasting this northern hemisphere,

spiralling for pure pleasure through this night of nights
scented with brine and silverlings and sea lavender
before, bored with the same old rum-snoring sailors,
going off to search for its own kind,
to breeze through an East Wynd casement,

curling in with the night air, sweet-brewed,
so Elspeth Deuchar's mouth falls open by an inch,
she's dancing flamenco in a cramasie-bodiced dress
for a ballroom of unicorns; her carriage idles
ready to sweep her over the hills. Her lips

feel slippery as honey. She rubs her toes
along her lover's instep: he purrs in his sleep
halfway across the Grand Canyon on a high wire,
hands waving swords of yellow gladioli
while Sarah Scourie's sweater, knitted with sore bent fingers,

unrolls, a blue-grey sea of syllables, row after row
wave upon wave, the true story of her long life.
And Fiona's stubborn bread dough, knuckled under, laughs and is a baby.
And stump-legged Sandie roars on the rise and swoop of a force ten,
white walls slamming the deck, breath torn out of his ribcage,

his red hair on end in pointy arrows, yelling
Montevideo! Tierra del Fuego! Lower Largo! And each
time the swell yoiks him up like the best joke he's ever heard.
And the minister's wife finds the whale tooth lost in that fire,
holds it in her hands again, smooths over her father's scrimshaw lullaby

'*out of the strong came forth sweetness*' then puts it to her mouth.
And Jamie's long-gone mother whispers *hushie-ba, hushie-ba, wheesht now*
as he leaps like a dog into the soap and soda shallows of her lap.
At first light the Manitou sails, leaving no sound or trace
in the milky water; and clustering around the proud

bare-breasted lady where she commands the prow, nuzzling
those salt-polished pointy hives, there's an odd, airborne smudge of those
surprised to wake and find themselves so far from gorse and heather and seaswept gardens,
from their own beds: light-headed a little, even dizzy, from
so much sweet feasting out of sorrow.

Newala

Letter from my son

He saw the fever tree first,
forty years higher than in my photograph
then the house, red-roofed,
low built against the heat,
its white veranda
as if untouched –
and the plains below
clear to the Mozambique border.
Close up, he saw those steps
gap-toothed, crumbling.
Wrote: *something shivered and crept in me.*

In the rainy season of the fourth year of my life
I would lie under that roof, heart's yammer
a spoon knocking in a tin bowl,
a man beating a dog.
Door opening into the dark over an invisible drop
I would look at water poured into my glass,
listen to ghosts drinking.

The photograph brought him here
to my father in his straw hat,
the dogs slumped in the cool
beside the wall: my mother, stunned by the sun.
Something shivers and creeps in me.

Now I am walking the path towards the steps.
Look, I say, pulling him forward,
welcome us. I raise my hands.
Your unexpected guests.

Spending One Day with Patrick Kavanagh

I took the train from Cork that day
to quell the chewing voice that said
I have to go and see that man
before I'm dead.

Dublin's air was oyster grey, the river like an unmade bed.

Between us we had what we had to say. A gull
sat a while upon his head.
Though it turned chill I had to stay;
the two of us unwashed, unfed.

And no one ever knew that way
the years of speechlessness I shed.

Brendan Kennelly told the story on Radio 4 of a woman who had travelled all the way from Cork by train to sit beside the statue of Patrick Kavanagh.

KATHRYN MARIS is the author of *The Book of Jobs* (Four Way Books, 2006). She received a Pushcart Prize and an Academy of American Poets award, and has published poems in *Poetry Review, Poetry, The Harvard Review, Modern Poetry in Translation* and several anthologies. She teaches creative writing at Kingston University and Morley College in London.

'The Tall Thin Tenor', 'On Returning a Child To Her Mother at the Natural History Museum', 'Hilary Has Left the Building, Unless She Hasn't' and 'Doubting Thomas' first appeared in *Poetry London.* 'This Is a Confessional Poem' was a runner-up in the Troubadour Poetry Competition and appeared on the Troubadour website.

Some statistics on these poems: 71 per cent were written at artists' residencies; 57 per cent were the results of exercises set by Mimi Khalvati in her legendary Versification class at the Poetry School; and 100 per cent are poems I consider to be 'British Poems', by which I mean they are often quasi-formal or use blank verse; they tend to have clear narratives; the speakers are *of* the world rather than outside it; and irony is pervasive. My 'American Poems' are more abstract, psychological and spare, owing much to Wallace Stevens, Louise Glück and Emily Dickinson. Neither style of poem is more 'authentic' for me. After spending what is, by now, a third of my life in England, I like to think I'm somewhat culturally bilingual.

As for the individual poems. I wrote 'Doubting Thomas' after opening a hotel Bible to chapter 20 in the Gospel of John while looking for a 'bedtime story' for my daughter. I thought of a man called Tom who'd once rejected me, and it occurred to me to merge him with Jesus's disciple. The title character of 'The Tall Thin Tenor' was inspired in appearance by the tenor Ian Bostridge, even though the role of the emperor Nero in *L'incoronazione di Poppea* is generally not sung by a tenor. This fictitious narrative examines disloyalty and abandonment, themes I address again in 'Knowledge Is a Good Thing'. 'On Returning a Child To Her Mother at the Natural History Museum' was an experiment in writing an ostensibly autobiographical narrative in which the voice and tone of the speaker are overtly not my own. This is the reverse of my usual approach, which is to tell a *fiction* with my 'real' voice. 'This Is a Confessional Poem' is simultaneously a send-up of the 'confessional' genre and a genuine confession. But the speaker says she's a 'terrible, terrible liar' and is possibly not to be believed. As someone who is allergic to sentimental love poems, I nonetheless set out to write a tender and unironic love poem with 'If You Relive a Moment You Cannot Outlive It'. 'Hilary Has Left the Building, Unless She Hasn't', on the other hand, approaches elegy. It's about one of my students, a very gifted poet, who took her own life, and was in a coma when the poem was written.

Knowledge Is a Good Thing

My mind is open,
so the devil can get in.

We speak in the rhythm
of catechism.

'Look at this.'
'But it is *His*.'

'What's his is yours.
Look in the drawers.'

'I'm forbidden
to know what's in them.'

'You're his wife.
Dig up his life.'

'Will I despair
at what's in there?'

'Better to know
than be in limbo.'

'That may be,
but remember the tree?'

'The world was built
on sin and guilt.'

'If that's true
it's thanks to you.'

*

He was victorious
for I was curious.

And there was no pardon
in the garden

where I sat
'til He came back.

Hilary Has Left the Building, Unless She Hasn't

Hilary did something to her house:
no one knows exactly *what*
she did, but it is wrecked
and no one can enter for fear
of the whole thing collapsing.

The firemen stood outside her door
for a few solid days
but they left to save another house
on which they could use their hatchets –
and that had a better outcome.

Her parents and friends have knocked
at the door gingerly,
as have employees of the council,
and even a devious estate agent
who saw a plot of land at the ready.

I, too, knocked,
questioning her, as a teacher must,
and though it had always been in her nature
to give me the correct answers,
this time there was nothing.

The matter remains to this day:
if she is still in the house
there can be no hasty decisions;
but if she has left the house
the structure can be razed without regret.

If You Relive a Moment You Cannot Outlive It

I have relived the same moment of happiness
so many times in my mind, it has taken a toll
on my physical health. As a consequence
of drinking the same glass of vodka year after
year, I've developed what the French call
crise de foie, which is apparently an early sign
of liver failure. We've had passion without
respite, which has been tiring,
not to mention all the pregnancies –
and my weight gain has not been insubstantial.
I have suffered chronic headaches
due to the inhalation of cat piss wafting eternally
from the stairwell. I have gone deaf from
listening to blues and have also become depressed.
Is it possible to sue the past for medical damages?
I hope so because I have an ulcer
from the love I felt for you; and next week
I have an appointment with the cardiologist
because the prolonged stress and anxiety over what
you felt for me, which seemed to be nothing,
induced an arrhythmia so serious I have sometimes
required a crash cart. I should let the moment go
in the hopes my health improves, as one gives up
smoking or introduces a multivitamin,
but what's the point of living without any joy?

The Tall Thin Tenor

The tall thin tenor sings
The tall thin tenor sings to the young soprano
The young soprano sings the part of Poppea
The young woman Poppea has seduced the king
The tall thin tenor is king
The young soprano Poppea becomes the new young queen
The young soprano replaces the old queen Ottavia
The old queen Ottavia sings of replacement

The tall thin tenor sings over the soprano
The tall thin tenor sings over her to his small thin wife
His small thin wife holds a child in the stalls
His thin wife holds their quiet daughter
His small wife sings quietly to their daughter
The small wife is quiet when the queen sings

On Returning a Child to Her Mother at the Natural History Museum

Hello my name is Kathryn and I've come
here to return your daughter, Emily.
She told me you'd suggested that she look
around upstairs in 'Earthquakes and Volcanoes',
then meet you and her brothers in the shop.
You know that escalator leading to
the orb? It's very long and only goes
one way, you can't turn back. She asked me if
I knew the way back down and would we come
with her into the earthquake simulator –
that reproduction of the grocery shop
in Kobe, where you see the customers
get thrown around with Kirin beer and soy
sauce, things like that. She told us stuff about
your family. Apparently you had
a baby yesterday! That can't be right:
you're sitting here without one and my God
your stomach's flat! She also said she'd had
an operation in the hospital
while you were giving birth one floor below.
I know, I know: kids lie and get confused,
mine do that too. She talks a lot. She's fat.
She may not be an easy child to love.
I liked her, though. I liked her very much,
and having her was great, the only time
all day my daughter hasn't asked me for
a dog! We got downstairs and funnily
enough we found your middle son. He ran
to us upset and asked us where you were.
But here you are – exactly where you said –
the shop! Don't worry: I don't ever judge
a mother. Look at me: my daughter drank
the Calpol I left out when she was two;
I gave my kids Hundreds and Thousands once
for dinner while I lay down on the floor,
a wreck. I know you well! Here's Emily.

Doubting Thomas

Call me Infidel, or just call me Tom.
Call me handsome, call me cold, call me bitter, call me cad
call me No-Better-Than-Judas-Iscariot
call me bachelor, call me saint, call me numb.

I was abused, I was married, I took pills, I was left,
I was in love, I was a liar, I was a drunk, I was in debt,
I wrote a book, I had some fame, then I was dead,
'til I was saved, I slept around, I was too young, I was bereft.

You are good, you are beautiful, you are kind, you forgive,
you are loving, you are smart, you're adored and you are brave.

There's no one else. It isn't you. I'm circumspect. I'm full of doubt.
It wouldn't work. We're not alike. I don't know what I want.

Call me weak, call me ingrate, call me 'once bitten, twice shy'.
Call me anything, but please don't say I make you want to die.

This Is a Confessional Poem

I am guilty of so much destruction it hardly matters
any more. There are so many thank-you notes I never wrote
that sometimes I'm relieved by the deaths of would-be
recipients, so I can finally let go of the shame.
I was awful to someone who was attached to the phrase
'social polish' as though she'd acquire it through repetition.
I took an overdose at a child's sixth birthday party.
I was born in a country which some have called
the Big Satan. I abandoned the country for one
that is called the Little Satan. I wished ill on a woman
who has known me for years and yet never remembers
who I am – and now she's involved in a public scandal.
I have been at parties where I was boring.
I have been at parties where I was deadly boring.
I have worn the wrong clothes to sacraments, not
for lack of outfits, but for a temporary failure of taste.
I'm a terrible, terrible liar, and everything I say is full of
misrepresentation. I once knew a very sweet girl
who stabbed herself in the abdomen seven times.
She believed she was evil and thought seven was a holy number.
Besides that she was sane, and told me her tale
out of kindness – because guilt recognises guilt,
the way a mother can identify her own child.
I met her in a class called 'Poetry Therapy'
in which the assignment was to complete this statement:
When one door closes, another opens.
I wrote: *At the end of my suffering there was a door,*
making me guilty of both plagiarism and lack of imagination.
I was the vortex of suffering: present, future and retroactive
suffering. The girl tried to absolve me.
'Don't be Jesus,' she said. 'There are enough around here.'
I know I should thank her if she's alive,
but I also know it's unlikely I'll rise to the task.

M.R. PEACOCKE was born in 1930. She read English at Oxford – though she spent more time on music. She travelled, taught, married, had four children, trained and worked as a counsellor, before moving to rural Cumbria, where she kept a smallholding and planted trees. She has published four collections of poetry.

'Les Pompes Funèbres' was first published in *Artemis Poetry* and 'Seaside Stories' in *Poetry London*.

I find the making of poems difficult and necessary. I have written poetry since childhood, but did not attempt to publish until well into middle age. I was always plagued by the belief that I had nothing worth saying – and still am, but have moved from belief to agnosticism and get on with it.

I am a countrywoman, and my poems tend to have a rural context; but they are often rooted in memory and may serve as exorcism: if a recollection haunts me and I can get it adequately into words, it will leave me alone.

Now I am old, poetry has become essential as a method of exploring the processes of my life, for which nothing else seems to have prepared me. I find it difficult to read much, in poetry or anything else; but I'm constantly turning to the etymological dictionary, loving language for itself and for the way words carry their history with them. I return to certain poets: George Herbert, Edward Thomas, Seamus Heaney, Zbigniev Herbert in translation, Cavafy, sometimes Yeats, Donne, Tennyson; and certain American poets, notably Elizabeth Bishop and Lisel Mueller, a wonderful poet little known over here.

There are musicians in my family, and if I had the technical skill I would compose rather than write; but language is the instrument I have and that has a hold over me. I used to relish romantic language, but now increasingly I love the sounds and rhythms of demotic speech and its Old English ancestry. How to set a poem on the page, especially how to pace the silences, is an absorbing matter; and I can't discover what I really want to say until I find the right form. (One I construct for myself, seldom a traditional form.) Once I have established that, I feel relief and a kind of joy. George Herbert speaks for me: *And now in age I bud again: / After so many deaths, I live, and write.*

Les Pompes Funèbres

Black armbands. The end of the war, and London had gaps in it. We were taken to Kettner's, and had creamed tinned sweetcorn. And Sauternes: the first time I tasted wine. There were very old waiters holding napkins. I was ashamed because the lining of my coat was torn.

A Roget of cherry stones: Subdued reserved composed demure,
Needful indispensable essential de rigueur.

And later on in Paris. It is a quarter past one. In the grace of ancient poverty she selects, as usual, the horse-mince; and he, leaning beside her faded hat and having removed the menu, pours the little red.

Ah, the pearl grey assurance of knowing what may be spoken, how things should be done: time, place, style, act. A paper cloth. Ah, the dead.

Seaside Stories

How It Was

We might begin at the beginning
with our buckets and spades
our wooden spades and red tin buckets
and our watching mothers
our reliable smiling mothers
with sandwiches and tea

or else cut straight to the adventures
the games we played, the tricks
(and didn't we laugh) and move right on
(Oh Fred) (That smashing Jill)
to the war and the air raid warnings
and the times we nearly

We ponder by the double glazing
and think how best to start
because things Things have changed and if we
We could tell such stories

But the sea is first at the window
offering its fictions

Dog Days

Retired dogs leading
their ancient masters
in very clean shoes
to the sea, the sea
by way of benches
and letting them sit
if the weather smiles
for a breather

(a breather permits
the flock of recall
and some sweet relief
of the knees, the knees)
and when we have done
the green kiosk bench
with flaking paint, then
the Promenade

(some excellent stinks
on the Prom, the Prom)
benches two and three
and if we can make
the Point it will be
a very good day
old fella old gal
at your age, eh?

and a brief poke round
while they take their snooze
and a lovely dump
and a piss with Tom
Sandy Gertie Jack
(overweight maybe
but times we've had, eh?
roistering times)

Blue Hat

You never know do you: like
Miss Colebrook down there in her macintosh
her mac and her big white shoes
rolling at the lip of the tide. She went
rolypoly up a bit
and then rolypoly down on the ebb
just like that. The sea was calm.
Miss Colebrook too, they say perfectly calm.
You'd think she'd look distracted
wouldn't you but not at all. She just laid
her blue hat on the shingle
with her stick at right angles to the sea
(they were there in the morning)
and went on walking down. And that's a fact.
She'd nothing under her mac.

Perhaps if we'd waved when the blue hat passed
or if we'd said good evening

Late Season

Oh lonely sea that has lost its wits
old sea tremulous in autumn heat
bluish and uncertain and later
chafing and irascible Payne's grey
pilfering fugitive and shifty
and always still to do still to do

its allotments where nothing grows
its pottering places and glory holes
and constructions and deconstructions
and trophies and accumulations –
by the waters of Albion we may
sit down we shall yes we can manage

Child's Play

Humming Top

A big hand weighs on the plunger
and pumps, stiffly at first
then fast and faster, lifts away
and there's my rackety top, changed,
humming like a planet,
flying and still, all its colours spinning
to one that hasn't a name.

How can it end now it's begun?
It does, though. There isn't a hand
that knows how to stop the stopping.
It's starting to weary,
and wag, and its colours
unravel again till, crash, there it is
by the chair leg, a striped tin thing.

Doll

Somebody cobbled her up, pale doll.
Tallow legs too long, each ending
at a strapped cloth shoe. Lampshade frock.
Arms with uncertain joints.
Somebody's rifled her pining head,
picked at her stitches, cockled her,
tossed her about, poked holes.

She can't stand up she can't sit down
She's stupid and plain
She can't tell fibs and she can't die.
She's for pinching and teasing
and smacking and squeezing
and squashing and biting
and hurting and hating
so shut her in the cupboard,
leave her in the dark 'cause she won't cry,
she won't say a word.

Rocking Horse

He's planted full stretch in the dapple
of the summerhouse that has three steps
and white paint gone to flake, showing
the pink and pudding brown.

I climb up one, two, three, to visit
his scratched black hooves and grey rosettes.
He's too tall to ride. His crimson eye
won't turn to me. The floorboards creak.

I offer him grass on my flat palm
the way you feed the milkman's horse
but his wooden nose ignores it,
snuffing the horizon.

One day the garden's changed, stretching
far and bare as Arabia, summerhouse gone,
rocking horse stolen away, forever
lost in the empty quarter.

Shall We Dance?

Dew almost frost. It's the heeltap
of summer, October's pourriture,
and drunken bumblebees are plunged
head down in buddleia nectar,
stuck to the narrow goblets, trembling
or sometimes tumbled to the yellow
of aftermath, helpless, signalling
prayers with a hooky leg.
What shall we do about the mess?

Supposing you were to pick this last
buttonhole of blowsy Albertine,
it would shed its ruffles. Reds
of the season are liverish,
apricots blotchy, pinks insipid
and no rhythm among the greens.
Sun looks bloodless, serving
at the final banquet (remember
ancient waiters at the Deux Magots?).

A few small flies still reel
among the diagonals of light
where leaves leak like inverted plops
of air from goldmouth fishes,
and there isn't a bird, not one
whose voice is not derelict; so, light
a lucky match among the trash,
and watch how sap still forces
bubbles out of a chopped branch.

Thirteenth Night

If you're wise, an angel whispered to us,
you'll go home by a different route.

Which we did. The long way round. It takes years.
People eye our rags and tell us

So what did you achieve. Precious little.
A wild goose chase after a star.

Pay no attention to angels. Listen,
the rafters drip, the panes are smashed,

your children have sold all the furniture
and the mattresses skip with mice.

Watch long enough and the stars start jumping.
We change our story every day

and people listen, hoping for a clue
but what they hear's not what we said.

Finding your way home: that's the pilgrimage.
Gone yesterday here tomorrow.

The hills lay down their muzzles at our fire.
We are obliged to eat rubies.

What's left? Still something crazy in the feet,
wanting to die, wanting to dance.

Jug

Mugshot of jug: paunchy larderpod,
        of the earth, earthy; smudged with morning;
texture of apple (October Russet); half-shine.
        A spider had crocheted a pale drape
        in the handle and left off, the way
people of the house had given up and were gone
        and were nowhere; but the jug still sat
        in this emptied somewhere, possessing
its soul in patience. I lifted it down, a shawl
        of dust around its shoulder. Shadow
        lay at the depth like a tarnished coin.
I washed it, and thought jug heaven would be cream and cool,
        its songsound all vowel; and watch it now,
        sweating a little but ready for milk
or rain; and yet it's like a stray dog that wants you
        to take it on: hope almost bursts it.
        It needs time to become its new self
accustomed to light, and service, and company.
        So here it can sit in the kitchen,
        good jug, the quiet bulging inside,
a whole cruseful of air: that'll last me: plenty.

DAVID SHOOK attended graduate school at Oxford, finishing with distinction. His work has appeared in *Agenda, Oxford Magazine, Poetry, World Literature Today,* and elsewhere. His chapbook of translations of Zapotec poet Víctor Terán is available from the Poetry Translation Centre. Shook lives in Los Angeles, where he edits *Molossus*.

My interest in these poems, ultimately, is with the multiplicity of voices that narrate my experience as a poet and human, having grown up an American in Mexico City (and elsewhere) and now living in Los Angeles, the second most populous Mexican city in the world. My writing is an attempt to subvert the systems in place for understanding my experience in the city, which I don't believe can be herded neatly into any unified narrative. As Edward Said said in an unpublished lecture from 2001, 'Hence the alternative notion, that the world is incomplete, in the process of becoming, a magnificent series of fragments, certainly uncontainable by reductive schemes.'

'Postcard from Weslaco' is based on a story of a Mexican friend who immigrated illegally to Chicago, along the Coyote highways. 'Postcard from El Paso' is based on another story that an illegal immigrant told me, explaining why he enjoys his current job as a day laborer, waiting for work outside the hardware store.

The real Silvestre Adán, a native speaker of Guerrero Nahuatl, lives in San Agustín Oapan, a village in Guerrero, Mexico, that has been continually inhabited since before the time of Christ. I learned much about the lives of contemporary indigenous Mexicans from him, as well as what I know of contemporary Nahuatl, swimming in the Rio Balsas, feeding his cattle, and tending his watermelon orchard.

Tule is a 2000-year-old tree outside Oaxaca, Mexico; this poem is my own offering to the tree, which is decorated with offerings for religious holidays. 'Peluqueria Poema' is the name of a hair salon in Oaxaca, written in this instance as a tribute to the Los Angeles hairdressers that sponsors my work.

My own understanding of poetry is always in interaction with other poets, poetries, and society at large – other magnificent fragments – and in this sense I feel my work in particular dialogue with that of the Mexican poets I translate: Isthmus Zapotec poets Víctor Terán and Víctor de la Cruz, Francisco Hernández, Hugo Hiriart, Tedi López Mills, Moisés Náufrago, and Classical Nahuatl poet Tecuani. These poems also converse with the poets who have taught me, in person and in reading, among them past and present Oxford Poets Jamie McKendrick, Jenny Lewis, and Jane Draycott.

Postcard from Weslaco

You know how this begins: after two days
they demand more money than we agreed on,
& what can we do, right? We're out in the
desert in a town made of tents, cinder
blocks, & semi-trucks. We're thinking of ways
to find cash, cause they put what we eat on
a tab too. Even though you did what we
told you, like my wife did what we told her,
they still wanted more. He was vomiting
by then, thin pink strings that striped the sand
outside our plastic tarp. He heaved at night.
I told him we should wait it out, till something
changed – & I shouldn't have let him demand
we leave. I'll just say it. Your husband died.

Four Ash Fall Questions

1 The Volcanologist

Hasn't ashed like this since Kennedy's visit in '62,
an army of tephra stretched across the polluted sky,

soldiers of coarse & fine ash, lapilli sergeants &
agglomerate commanders linger behind their troops.

Popocatepetl's ash cone swells, the city is too busy
for tuff to cement. The pale yellow of early ashfall grays,

the city is perfumed with sulfur. All flights suspended,
air tense with tephric static. Asthmatic children

cough in chorus, smokers smoke inside.
Will tomorrow bring your Bishop's ring?

2 The Nurse

If your throat is the cone that ends in
your rocky lips, your intestines have been

swollen deep within the earth for days.

Lava burns your esophagus. You vomit rocks.
No one will wipe the filth from your lips.

Who comforts the mountains when they are sick?

3 The Mango Vendor

The streets are salted with ash
like the first day of each new year,

without the newspaper skins of
Mexican fireworks. The boys

with their bottles & rags do
so good their pockets clink.

Mangos sell like normal, no
tabloid gossip here no rush.

Two for one today, swollen with
real rain. Why not try, why not

bite into the only reds & oranges
not dulled by ash?

4 Boy in Álvaro Obregón

The sun burns orange through
the haze, the color of ripe peach

flesh near its pit, bar flash
neon, the glow of heated

metal, the lit tip of your cigarette,
god. When will you lift it,

lift it from the ashtray of the valley?

Silvestre Adán

As carpenter

I hewed six pews from the pine logs we netted in the Balsas,
chiseled the wind into the robes of the saints in San Miguel,

carved lips & brows, hollowed nostrils. Sawed soft wood
into tables, sanded moisture from its skin. Seldom chairs.

Boxes for the dead, when boxes. Like Jorge's son:
body bloated with the river's spit, eyes glazed with mezcal.

Still, I doctor the stubbed toes of Santiago,
massage Juan Buatista's cracked palms with heated sap.

Rub ash from their singed feet,
admire joints hinged tighter than my own.

Postcard from El Paso: Night Shift at the Hotdog Factory

Blood is only blood when warm, when
cold it congeals to simple mess,
to a nightly shift & a thin
wad of cash to wire back. I dress
in the same stained jeans each night, the was-blood
& soapy water soak through to my thighs.
The butcher's apron is prop. Soured cud
& matted hair leave on my shoes. Guys
like me are a dime a dozen
so I can't complain: it's work &
work is money. Lately I've been
doing doubles, since Luis got canned.

Work's in our blood – in blood – you used to say.

My love to Chueco, Maria, José –

Offerings to Tule

1

Through the branches
light stripes its thumbtip horns.
The dome of its skull is the base of
a pitcher retching its gelatinous dregs
at the speed of sap. Blood drips from
the neck. The ants that live along
the roots circle drops like roundabouts.
The priest will leave it hanging till
its eyes dry, till its lids cave like
a womb post-partum.

2

Over a thin branch, xylem still pliable, a pair
of small shoes hang tied by their laces like a
phone wire taunt in miniature. Their feet turn
to dirt inside wool socks, in the earth beneath Tlalixtac.

3

A trumpet like an artificial limb,
a brass & copper branch, the mouth of
a tree that after two-thousand years
has not yet evolved to speech.

The Rest of the Cow

Its body in the butcher shop, its
tongue, too. Its mouth an empty
home papered in cud.
The butcher's dog will eat
its heart, relish its saltiness, the
heart that beat like a trout
fresh on the floor of a boat
as the knife approached its neck.
Which of its seven stomachs
tensed first, which will make
the least bitter stew?

Peluqueria Poema

for The Hive Los Angeles

There is a carpet here of hair.
There is a heaven of curled clouds.
Lice praise me with their harps.

Neck, this is breeze. Breeze, neck.
I introduce cheekbones to sun,
I hide roots' climb towards light.

I've heard hair keeps growing after death,
but I've never styled a corpse. I fight years
with dye & foil, sweep the evidence away.

If some god knows how many hairs
we each have, I write his riddles with
my scissors.

RYAN VAN WINKLE is the Reader in Residence at the Scottish Poetry Library. He runs a 'Literary Cabaret' called the Golden Hour and is an editor at Forest Publications. His work has appeared in *New Writing Scotland, The American Poetry Review, AGNI and Northwords Now*. His first collection is published by Salt (2010). www.ryanvanwinkle.com

'It Is Summer and in Connecticut the Grill Is Grilling' was first published in *New Writing Scotland*: 26; 'They Tore the Bridge Down a Year Later' first appeared in *Northwords Now*; 'Gasoline' was placed second in the Ver Poetry Prize and 'My 100-year-old ghost' first appeared in *V: New International Writing from Edinburgh*. Grateful acknowledgements are made to the editors of these publications.

Naming sources or inspirations for poems can be difficult but I must admit to knowingly being a thief and can pinpoint source material to actual places, people or events. For instance, 'Knots' was only written because of a trip to a cabin in Loch Tay where the walls were decorated with examples of the mentioned knots. 'My 100-year-old ghost' is indebted to Bill McKibben's book, *The Age of Missing Information* (Random House, 2006). Specifically, McKibben wrote 'Why leave when you can live in a place you can understand and that understands you.' Reading this after I left my American home for my Scottish one resonated, and still does whenever I think of departing to a warmer country. Also, the lake originally cited in this poem is Unca's Lake in Southern Connecticut where I grew up. However, 'Unca' looks too much like a typo for Uncle. 'Ode For a Rain From Death Row' was inspired by Kenny Richey's quote. Richey, a Scot who moved to America when he was eighteen, had been embroiled in the politics of death row since his conviction for murdering a two-year-old girl in Ohio in July of 1986. Allegedly he was trying to burn down his ex-girlfriend's apartment. For over two decades he lived on death row in Ohio and had appealed his sentence numerous times. In January 2006 Richey gave this quote during an interview with the *Observer*. While these facts certainly informed the poem, I cannot say it is about Richey any more than I can say he is an innocent man. For the record, in December 2007 he accepted a plea bargain which led to his release from death row and return to Scotland, where he has been arrested several times since.

'They Tore the Bridge Down a Year Later' is also informed by real-life events. In October of 1990, Falyssa Van Winkle, a ten-year-old girl from Lake Charles, Louisiana, was raped, murdered and left under a bridge in Newton County. This crime was mentioned briefly in Dina Temple-Raston's *A Death in Texas* (Holt Paperbacks, 2003). Falyssa is not related to me. 'The day he went to war' was written at the beginning of the current Iraq war. It references a Frank Zappa song.

It Is Summer and in Connecticut the Grill Is Grilling

Grandma roasts swordfish on the grill while smoking her death down.
Dad brings brown bags bursting with ripe tomatoes, zucchini, eggplants
from his prescribed garden. They eat off a long picnic table;
the same table grandma danced on in that impossible photo from the 50s
before she broke her hip.

The table has been painted many things: argument red,
family yellow, divorce brown. Today, it's just her favourite blue.
I think the corn will be sweet and its green husks will wait in the trash
for dinners' meaty remains. Eric won't touch the fish, neither will dad.
Burgers must be cooked.

They do not know the time in my zone.
Ghosts are in the sockets and they write to me of food: of Thanksgiving dinners,
Christmas hams, summer hot dogs. I could write about the yellow rings on the sheets,
the teeth in the pipes, all the light bulbs which have gone missing, the hair of the dog,
the colors of the rain I wear, the plaque on benches, the voices behind walls.
I send a letter, later, about nothing.

Falling #71

Gray hairs bush around his temple.
His wife says she doesn't notice,
doesn't mind, anyway.
And he thinks, well,
which is it, darling?

Knots

She is a god of knots.
His socks are Spanish Bows and
in the night the doors are secured
with a tight Sheep Shank, china cups

hang on Artillery Loops
and she twists her own hair
when she worries, pulls it
over and around and then through

and around again until it hangs
in a Jury Mast and some nights,
when the door is tight, she gets me
in a Carrick Bend and I am told

about the old Bill Hitch
and all the time I hope
she's tied herself up
enough to stay the storm.

They Tore the Bridge Down a Year Later

I

I found her in a blue dress
beneath the old wooden bridge
with ropes round her wrists,
her neck, her ankles.

It's how we would tie a hog.
When there was money
for that type of thing.

Her hair was perfect
the day she left Beaumont
but, by the time Powell got her to Texas,
her dress looked like it had caught
the wrong side of a horse.

I remember they told me
Falyssa Van Winkle was ten,
and she got raised
a little north of here.

They said she went to buy peanuts
at some flea market in Beaumont
and her mother watched Falyssa go,
kept hawking clay ashtrays
and heavy magnifying glasses;
nothing fancy, just stuff
people sometimes need.

Five hours later Falyssa
was under the bridge I used to spit off
and Powell was cleaning his mobile home,
readying to drive north.

II

A year later the new bridge went up.
All clean cable and wire,
so the cars could drive too fast
and my boy and I couldn't sit there,
let the water pass.

As a kid, I'd rest on the splintered rail,
protected in the strong shade of the Cyprus Pines,
drop pennies or spit onto the frogs of Cow Creek
back when it ran clear.

But they said a good car couldn't cross it.
So I guess the children
who used to throw pennies, spit,
had to find something new.

I can still see the old bridge,
the pennies rusting in water.

III

Nowadays I don't pass the creek much.
There is no reason to walk my quiet boy
across metal into Louisiana.

If the bridge I knew still stood
maybe I could bring my boy down,
tell him the lawn can wait. Tell him

his father wants to pass the time,
make him talk.
But the bridge is not there any more.

And Falyssa's bag of salted peanuts
has run down, met the big river.
That last thing of hers,
heading out for the open ocean.

IV

She was from over the border in Lake Charles.
I used to like the song about it,
could play it a little on the guitar.

My boy found the scratched thing up in the attic
with some photos of me and his mom
and he asked me to play.

I like to think I could have taken him to the creek,
brought a fishing pole, that cheap guitar,
made something happen,
before he too cuts out for some sea.

I told him I couldn't remember anything.
Maybe I can't.

Somebody told me Powell made it into the papers,
said his last words were, 'I am ready for my blessing.'

Next time my boy gets into the attic
I want to follow him up, tell him,
So am I.

Gasoline

A week ago I spilled
a can of gasoline onto the dirt
floor of the barn.

A gallon or so soaked into the earth.
Since then, I've had headaches,
can't catch my balance.

And I can still smell the gas
from more than twenty yards away.
It reminds me of hitching west

and this ride I hooked
in the back of a truck
the color of rust.

When I shook the driver's hand he smiled.
His teeth looked like a caterpillar
and I knew I was beat.

The guy kept all these rags back there,
soaked in gasoline. It was warm
and I fell asleep in a cocoon of reek.

When I came to, it was almost time
to get out. I could feel caterpillars on me,
thought I was going to suffocate.

He said the free ride was over, it was only a matter of time,
and I didn't wish to be out west,
didn't care to sit in any more cars with strangers and talk
about the pace or weather back east.

I tried to lose the smell in a stream,
thought I sent it upriver, away
like father, the attic, his ties.

Ode for a Rain from Death Row

The rain is a cold, clean prayer,
the only light I want to see.
I say it still rains on her

like it rains on the bars and streets
somewhere outside the walls.
And in the rain, she is always twenty,

her shoes always candy-red Converse,
her jeans always damped to her thighs,
her mouth never parted from mine.

She hasn't pressed her lips to glass
since the fire; the ashes are back to ashes, the dust
follows dust, the spring rain powders her arms

and evaporates in the stare of the sun.
And this rain is the only light I want to see.
A mist that kisses till my socks are sponge,

till the fire fizzles and baby is back again
cooing with hot-chocolate-warm hands.
Before I die I want to stand outside,

birth-naked, let the lord soak me.
But options and pardons are gone.
The priest only offers a glass where

my throat wants a holy rain that pours
in sheets and hoods and lasts for forty days,
till it floods, and floats my sins away.

my dearest wish before I die is to stand outside in Scottish rain and to feel it soak me.

Kenny Richey, Death Row, Ohio

Discreet

Anyone could have killed him, anything on the street.
Cigarettes, booze, a penny dropped,
the wind, the rain, maybe the sun or sleet.

It wasn't our fists or the flash of our feet.
I couldn't hear, but it wasn't the push down the stairs.
Anything could have killed him. Anything on the street.

It wasn't the ride in the trunk, or even the fire, the heat.
Anyone could have killed him. But I guess it was Joe.
With the bat. Not the wind, rain, sun, or sleet.

Mike would say dudes should keep discreet,
and Bill would say we didn't ask for his spit or his rag.
Anything could have killed him, anything on the street.

Everyday he begged like we owed him, hand out for a piece
and if it wasn't us it would have been something else:
the wind, the rain, maybe the sun or sleet.

And I guess the cops see it all the time, down on that beat
and if they care it hasn't made the papers or buzzed the air.
If it did, folks'd say anything could kill a man on the street;
could have been the wind, the rain. Maybe the sun or sleet.

My 100-year-old ghost

My 100-year-old ghost
sits up with me when the power cuts,

tells about the trout at Unkee's Lake,
the wood house burned on the hill.

He says he was intimate
with every leaf of grass.

Wore one hat for Griswold,
another for his own field,

the possibilities of the century laid out;
an endless string of fishing pools.

But they never got ahead of my ghost –
he took them like cows, one at a time,

never lusted for the color of trout
in a pool a mile away.

He knew from the smoke in the sky
Mrs. Johnson was starting supper

and, in March, when the candles appeared,
he knew Bobby's boy had died.

My ghost only ever had one bar
where the keeper didn't water his drinks,

nor did he feel the need to hide his moth cap,
his potato clothes, or scrub himself birth pink.

My ghost tells me there was a time
you'd look out and not find a Dairy Queen.

You could sit on your porch a whole life,
and never, ever, think about China.

Sometimes I see my ghost
bringing cut sunflowers to his wife

and it seems so simple.
Then, sometimes, it is dark

he's just in from work and Griswold says
they ain't going to raise his pay.

And even back then the power went out,
long nights when they had no kerosene.

And my ghost tries to sell me on simpler times:
the grass soft, endless –

lampless nights,
pools of crickets singing.

The day he went to war

was bright, white and clean; an advertisement
for fresh laundry, lady things, or whatever.

we watched him from joe's garage, our music clanging;
hub caps and tin cans thrown against cement.

we watched his mother watch the car that took him,
saw her wave at nothing, then, we took it from the top:
one, two, a – one two three four